PASTA
SAUCES

PASTA
SAUCES

ELIZABETH MARTIN

HERMES HOUSE

ACKNOWLEDGEMENTS

The author and publishers would like to thank Kathryn Keegan for being the hand model
and Viners (0181 450 8900) for providing the saucepans. The photographs of Italy on
pages 10, 22, 36, 54, 70 and 80 were reproduced with the permission of Carah Boden
(copyright © Carah Boden).

This edition published by Hermes House
an imprint of
Anness Publishing Limited
Hermes House
88-89 Blackfriars Road
London SE1 8HA

A CIP catalogue record for this book is available from the British Library

Publisher Joanna Lorenz
Project Editor Clare Nicholson
Designer David Rowley
Jacket Design Peter Butler
Photographer David Armstrong

Front cover illustrates variation of Spaghetti with Mixed Mushroom and Basil Sauce

Typeset by MC Typeset Limited

© Anness Publishing Limited 1994, 1996, 2000

Previously published as part of the Creative Cooking Series, Classic Pasta Sauces

1 3 5 7 9 10 8 6 4 2

Measurements
Three sets of equivalent measurements have been provided in the recipes here,
in the following order: Metric, Imperial and American. It is essential that units of
measurement are not mixed within each recipe. Where conversions result in
awkward numbers, these have been rounded for convenience, but are accurate
enough to produce successful results.

Contents

Introduction

Pasta has always been the symbol of Italian food, and today delights the palates of many world wide.

It is probably the most versatile food and yet it is so simple, consisting of nothing more than a mixture of flour and water in its most basic form, or flour and egg, but it can be made in so many different shapes and served with a whole host of ingredients.

Pasta is now well known for being one of the healthiest natural foods, being low in fat and high in vitamins and carbohydrates. Served with plenty of vegetables and fish, it is a healthy part of a well-balanced diet. It is also very easy to digest, making it ideal for those with dietary problems. However, although pasta is in itself not fattening, it is wise to take note that the sauce it is served with will determine the calorific value of the whole dish.

In this book I have tried to create an array of sauces – some more complicated than others – to suit everyone. Most are so simple that they can be cooked in minutes, while a few need a little more preparation. But whichever you choose, remember, if you can't find any of the ingredients, then improvise, because I promise you anything is possible with pasta.

1 *tagliatelle* **2** *thin noodles (linguine)* **3** *ravioli* **4** *pasta spirals (fusilli)* **5** *pasta tubes (rigatoni)* **6** *pasta shells (gomiti rigati)* **7** *tortellini* **8** *pasta ears (orecchiette)* **9** *spaghetti* **10** *penne* **11** *pasta twists (spirali)* **12** *pasta rounds (castiglioni)* **13** *spaghetti tricolore* **14** *curly spaghetti (fusilli col buco)* **15** *pasta spirals (fusilli tricolore)* **16** *short pasta tubes (canneroni)* **17** *macaroni* **18** *curly lasagne*

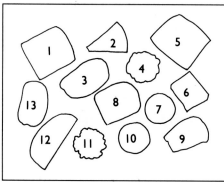

1 *Gruyère* **2** *dolcelatte* **3** *smoked mozzarella*
4 *mascarpone* **5** *Parmesan* **6** *fontina*
7 *herbed goats' cheese* **8** *Gouda* **9** *bel paese*
10 *mozzarella* **11** *curdled ricotta* **12** *Edam*
13 *roulé*

Choosing Pasta

There is an increasingly wide range of both fresh and dried pasta sold in supermarkets, as well as specialist shops and Italian delicatessens. Although none of these quite compare with fresh home-made pasta, they are still made with fine-quality ingredients.

Plain pasta – by far the most common – is made using durum flour and egg, but coloured pasta does add interest to a meal: green pasta (*verde*) is flavoured with spinach and red pasta (*rosso*) with tomatoes. You can even buy black pasta flavoured with cuttlefish ink. Wholemeal pasta is also available; it contains more fibre and consequently is more chewy in texture.

Illustrated on pages 6–7 are the shapes of pasta used in this book, with their names – however these vary simply because different regions of Italy have their own names for individual pasta shapes, as do the manufacturers.

There are no hard and fast rules on which pasta to use with which sauce, except that generally thin spaghetti suits the thinner sauces and shaped pastas suit the meatier sauces so that the bits get caught up in the pasta itself.

Cooking Pasta

Pasta is simple and easy to cook if you follow a few basic rules. It needs to be cooked in plenty of boiling water – allow 3 litres/5¼ pints water for each 450 g/1 lb of pasta.

1 Fill the pan with cold water and add about 1 tbsp of salt.

2 Bring to a rolling boil. Add a dash of olive oil.

3 Add the pasta and stir with a wooden spoon to separate the pasta.

4 Bring back to a rolling boil. Continue boiling, stirring occasionally, allowing 2–5 minutes for fresh pasta or 8–12 minutes for dried, until the pasta is *al dente*, which means firm to the bite. Pasta should not be mushy and should still hold its shape well. If you're not quite sure, continue boiling and keep checking regularly.

5 Drain and toss in the pasta sauce.

Choosing Herbs

Herbs are considered a very important part of Italian cooking, giving fragrant flavours to all types of pasta sauces.

When choosing herbs, look for those with unblemished leaves, that smell fresh and give off a pleasant scent when you break one. You can chop the leaves finely or coarsely, or leave them whole to stir into sauces.

Basil: one of Italy's most famous herbs. For the sweetest flavour, use freshly grown basil in a pot.

Coriander: quite a strong flavour and looks like flat leaf parsley.

Dill: has a totally unique spicy, green taste. It goes well with fish, cream cheese and cucumber.

Oregano: a small-leaved herb with a delicate flavour, it is popular with Italian cooks.

Mint: a very common herb, this is used frequently in Italian cooking.

Parsley: popular in most cuisines, parsley is available as flat-leaved which has a better flavour than the more traditional curly variety.

Rosemary: gives a really strong Mediterranean taste.

Sage: an unforgettable flavour – quite powerful so use sparingly.

Thyme: the smallest leaved herb, it is extra pungent when fresh so use cautiously.

1 *rosemary* **2** *sage* **3** *mint* **4** *coriander* **5** *oregano* **6** *flat leaf parsley* **7** *basil* **8** *thyme* **9** *dill*

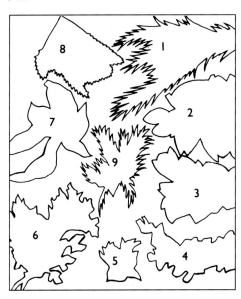

Traditional Sauces

This chapter is based on recipes, such as pesto sauce and carbonara, that conjure up the true taste of Italy. Obviously, the truly traditional recipes vary from region to region depending on the local ingredients, but I have chosen these sauces as they are real favourites everywhere.

Above   The Euganean hills, south of Padua, in spring.

Opposite   The Ponte Vecchio, Florence.

Ravioli with Four Cheese Sauce

This is a smooth cheesy sauce that coats the pasta very evenly.

SERVES 4

INGREDIENTS
350 g/12 oz ravioli
50 g/2 oz/¼ cup butter
50 g/2 oz/¼ cup plain flour
450 ml/¾ pint/2 cups milk
50 g/2 oz Parmesan cheese
50 g/2 oz Edam cheese
50 g/2 oz Gruyère cheese
50 g/2 oz fontina cheese
salt and freshly ground black pepper
chopped fresh flat leaf parsley, to garnish

1 Cook the pasta following the instructions in the introduction.

2 ▲ Melt the butter in a saucepan, stir in the flour and cook for 2 minutes, stirring occasionally.

3 ▲ Gradually stir in the milk until well blended.

4 ▲ Bring the milk slowly to the boil, stirring constantly until thickened.

5 ▲ Grate the cheeses and stir them into the sauce. Stir until they are just beginning to melt. Remove from the heat and season.

6 ▲ Drain the pasta thoroughly and turn it into a large serving bowl. Pour over the sauce and toss to coat. Serve immediately, garnished with the chopped fresh parsley

COOK'S TIP

If you cannot find all of the above cheeses, simply substitute your favourites.

Spaghetti alla Carbonara

This is a light and creamy sauce flavoured with bacon and lightly cooked eggs.

SERVES 4

INGREDIENTS
350 g/12 oz spaghetti
1 tbsp olive oil
1 onion, chopped
100 g/4 oz streaky bacon, rinded and diced, or pancetta
1 clove garlic, chopped
3 size, 3 eggs
300 ml/½ pint/1¼ cups double cream
salt and freshly ground black pepper
50 g/2 oz Parmesan cheese
chopped fresh basil, to garnish

1 Cook the pasta following the instructions in the introduction.

2 ▲ Heat the oil in a frying pan and fry the onion and bacon for 10 minutes until softened. Stir in the garlic and fry for a further 2 minutes, stirring occasionally.

3 ▲ Meanwhile, beat the eggs in a bowl, then stir in the cream and seasoning. Grate the Parmesan cheese and stir into the cream mixture.

4 ▲ Stir the cream mixture into the onion and bacon and cook over a low heat for a few minutes, stirring constantly until heated through. Season to taste.

5 Drain the pasta thoroughly and turn it into a large serving bowl. Pour over the sauce and toss to coat. Serve immediately, garnished with chopped fresh basil.

COOK'S TIP

Italians would use pancetta which is lightly cured but similar to streaky bacon. You can buy it in most supermarkets and delicatessens.

Pasta Twists with Classic Meat Sauce

This is a rich meat sauce which is ideal to serve with all types of pasta. The sauce definitely improves if kept overnight in the fridge. This allows the flavours time enough to mature.

SERVES 4

INGREDIENTS
450 g/1 lb minced beef
100 g/4 oz smoked streaky bacon, rinded
    and chopped
1 onion, chopped
2 sticks celery, chopped
1 tbsp plain flour
150 ml/¼ pint/⅔ cup chicken stock
    or water
3 tbsp/¼ cup tomato purée
1 clove garlic, chopped
3 tbsp chopped fresh mixed herbs, such as
    oregano, parsley, marjoram, chives or
    1 tbsp dried mixed herbs as an
    alternative
1 tbsp redcurrant jelly
350 g/12 oz pasta twists (spirali)
salt and freshly ground black pepper
chopped oregano, to garnish

1 Heat a large saucepan and fry the beef and bacon for about 10 minutes, stirring occasionally until browned.

2 Add the onion and celery and cook for 2 minutes, stirring occasionally.

3 ▲ Stir in the flour and cook for 2 minutes, stirring constantly.

4 ▲ Pour in the stock or water and bring to the boil.

COOK'S TIP

The redcurrant jelly helps to draw out the flavour of the tomato purée. You can use a sweet mint jelly or chutney instead.

5 ▲ Stir in the tomato purée, garlic, herbs, redcurrant jelly and seasoning. Bring to the boil, cover and simmer for about 30 minutes, stirring occasionally.

6 Cook the pasta following the instructions in the introduction. Drain thoroughly and turn it into a large serving bowl. Pour over the sauce and toss to coat. Serve immediately, garnished with chopped fresh oregano.

Pasta Tubes with Meat and Cheese Sauce

This combination of the two sauces complement each other perfectly.

SERVES 4

INGREDIENTS
For the Meat Sauce
1 tbsp olive oil
350 g/12 oz minced beef
1 onion, chopped
1 clove garlic, chopped
1 × 397 g/14 oz can chopped tomatoes
1 tbsp dried mixed herbs
2 tbsp tomato purée

For the Cheese Sauce
50 g/2 oz/¼ cup butter
50 g/2 oz/½ cup plain flour
450 ml/¾ pint/2 cups milk
2 egg yolks, size 3
50 g/2 oz/⅓ cup Parmesan cheese, freshly grated
salt and freshly ground black pepper

350 g/12 oz ridged pasta tubes (rigatoni)
fresh basil sprigs, to garnish

I ▲ To make the meat sauce, heat the oil in a large frying pan and fry the beef for 10 minutes, stirring occasionally until browned. Add the onion and cook for 5 minutes, stirring occasionally.

2 ▲ Stir in the garlic, tomatoes, herbs and tomato purée. Bring to the boil, cover and simmer for 30 minutes.

3 ▲ Meanwhile, to make the cheese sauce, melt the butter in a small saucepan, then stir in the flour and cook for 2 minutes, stirring constantly.

4 Remove the pan from the heat and gradually stir in the milk. Return the pan to the heat and bring to the boil, stirring occasionally until thickened.

5 ▲ Add the egg yolks, cheese and seasoning and stir until well blended.

6 ▲ Preheat the grill. Meanwhile, cook the pasta following the instructions in the introduction. Drain thoroughly and turn it into a large serving bowl. Pour over the meat sauce and toss to coat.

7 Divide the pasta among 4 flameproof dishes. Spoon over the cheese sauce and place under the grill until brown. Serve immediately garnished with fresh basil.

COOK'S TIP

Chopped canned tomatoes with added chopped herbs are now available from most supermarkets. If you prefer, simply substitute these and use half the quantity of dried herbs.

Curly Lasagne with Classic Tomato Sauce

A classic sauce that is simply delicious just served by itself.

SERVES 4

INGREDIENTS
2 tbsp olive oil
1 onion, chopped
2 tbsp tomato purée
1 tsp paprika
2 × 397 g/14 oz cans chopped tomatoes, drained
pinch of dried oregano
300 ml/½ pint/1¼ cups dry red wine
large pinch of caster sugar
salt and freshly ground black pepper
350 g/12 oz curly lasagne
Parmesan cheese shavings, to serve
chopped fresh flat leaf parsley, to garnish

1 ▲ Heat the oil in a large frying pan and fry the onion for 10 minutes, stirring occasionally until softened. Add the tomato purée and paprika and cook for 3 minutes.

2 ▲ Add the tomatoes, oregano, wine and sugar and season to taste, then bring to the boil.

3 ▲ Simmer for 20 minutes until the sauce has reduced and thickened, stirring occasionally.

4 Meanwhile, cook the pasta following the instructions in the introduction. Drain thoroughly and turn it into a large serving bowl. Pour over the sauce and toss to coat. Serve sprinkled with Parmesan cheese shavings and the chopped fresh parsley.

COOK'S TIP

If you cannot find curly lasagne use plain lasagne snipped in half lengthways.

Pasta Spirals with Pesto Sauce

A light, fragrant sauce like this dish gives a temptingly different taste.

SERVES 4

INGREDIENTS
For the Pesto Sauce
50 g/2 oz fresh basil leaves without
   the stalks
2 garlic cloves, chopped
2 tbsp pine nuts
salt and freshly ground black pepper
150 ml/¼ pint/⅔ cup olive oil
50 g/2 oz/⅓ cup Parmesan cheese,
   freshly grated

350 g/12 oz pasta spirals (fusilli)
freshly grated Parmesan cheese, to garnish
fresh basil sprigs, to garnish

1 Cook the pasta following the instructions in the introduction.

2 ▲ To make the pesto sauce, place the basil leaves, garlic, pine nuts, seasoning and olive oil in a food processor or liquidizer. Blend until very creamy.

3 Transfer the mixture to a bowl and stir in the Parmesan cheese.

4 Drain the pasta thoroughly and turn it into a large bowl. Pour over the sauce and toss to coat. Divide among serving plates and serve, sprinkled with the extra Parmesan cheese and garnished with fresh basil.

COOK'S TIP

Fresh basil is widely available from most greengrocers and supermarkets, either in growing pots or packets. If you buy a plant, remove the flowers as they appear so the plant grows more leaves.

   Pesto is best kept in a screw-topped jar in the fridge for up to 2 days. If you want to keep it a few days longer, cover the top with a thin layer of olive oil. This can be stirred into sauce when you are ready to add it to hot pasta.

Spaghetti with Meatballs

No Italian menu would be complete without meatballs. Serve these with a light green salad.

SERVES 4

INGREDIENTS
For the Meatballs
1 onion, chopped
1 garlic clove, chopped
350 g/12 oz minced lamb
1 egg yolk, size 3
1 tbsp dried mixed herbs
salt and freshly ground black pepper
1 tbsp olive oil

For the Sauce
300 ml/¹/2 pint/1¹/4 cups passata (see Cook's Tip)
2 tbsp chopped fresh basil
1 garlic clove, chopped
salt and freshly ground black pepper

350 g/12 oz spaghetti
fresh rosemary sprigs, to garnish
freshly grated Parmesan cheese, to serve

I ▲ To make the meatballs, mix together the onion, clove of garlic, lamb, egg yolk, herbs and seasoning until well blended.

2 ▲ Divide the mixture into 20 pieces and mould into balls. Place on a baking sheet, cover with cling film and chill for 30 minutes.

3 ▲ Heat the oil in a large frying pan and place the meatballs in it.

4 ▲ Fry the meatballs for about 10 minutes, turning occasionally until browned.

5 ▲ Add the passata, basil, garlic and seasoning to the pan and bring to the boil. Cover and simmer for 20 minutes until the meatballs are tender.

6 Meanwhile, cook the pasta following the instructions in the introduction. Drain thoroughly and divide it among 4 serving plates. Spoon over meatballs and some of the sauce. Garnish each portion with a fresh rosemary sprig and serve immediately with plenty of freshly grated cheese.

COOK'S TIP

Passata is available in jars, tins or cartons from specialist Italian grocery stores and most large supermarkets. It is made from sieved tomatoes, so if you cannot find any, drain and sieve canned tomatoes instead.
The meatballs can be made in advance. Place them on a baking sheet, cover with cling film and chill for about 1 day.

Meat Sauces

The Italians, like most people, enjoy their meat dishes, particularly the sausages and salamis of which there are many very tasty local varieties. Used in a pasta sauce, meat adds a strong flavour and richness. When combining meat with pasta, follow the rule that a little meat goes a long way.

Above   The harbour at Lazise, Lake Garda.

Opposite   The Euganean hills, south of Padua.

Pasta Spirals with Chicken and Tomato Sauce

A recipe for a speedy supper – serve this dish with a mixed bean salad.

SERVES 4

INGREDIENTS
1 tbsp olive oil
1 onion, chopped
1 carrot, chopped
50 g/2 oz sun-dried tomatoes in olive oil,
  drained weight
1 garlic clove, chopped
1 × 397 g/14 oz can chopped tomatoes,
  drained
1 tbsp tomato purée
150 ml/¼ pint/⅔ cup chicken stock
350 g/12 oz pasta spirals (fusilli)
225 g/8 oz chicken, diagonally sliced
salt and freshly ground black pepper
fresh mint sprigs, to garnish

1 ▲ Heat the oil in a large frying pan and fry the onion and carrot for 5 minutes, stirring occasionally.

2 ▲ Chop the sun-dried tomatoes and set aside.

3 ▲ Stir the garlic, canned tomatoes, tomato purée and stock into the onions and carrots and bring to the boil. Simmer for 10 minutes, stirring occasionally.

4 Cook the pasta following the instructions in the introduction.

5 ▲ Pour the sauce into a food processor or liquidizer and blend until smooth.

6 ▲ Return the sauce to the pan and stir in the sun-dried tomatoes and chicken. Bring back to the boil, then simmer for 10 minutes until the chicken is cooked. Adjust the seasoning.

7 ▲ Drain the pasta thoroughly and toss it in the sauce. Serve immediately, garnished with fresh mint.

COOK'S TIP

Sun-dried tomatoes are sold in jars soaked in vegetable or olive oil. The olive-oil soaked tomatoes do have a superior flavour. For extra flavour, fry the onion and carrot in 1 tbsp of the oil from the tomatoes.

Spaghetti with Bacon, Chilli and Tomato Sauce

This substantial sauce is a meal in itself, so serve as a warming winter supper.

SERVES 4

INGREDIENTS
1 tbsp olive oil
225 g/8 oz smoked streaky bacon, rinded and roughly chopped
350 g/12 oz spaghetti
1 tsp chilli powder
1 quantity Classic Tomato Sauce (see Curly Lasagne with Classic Tomato Sauce)
salt and freshly ground black pepper
roughly chopped fresh flat leaf parsley, to garnish

1 ▲ Heat the oil in a large frying pan and fry the bacon for about 10 minutes, stirring occasionally until crisp and golden.

COOK'S TIP

To lower the calorie content of this sauce, pour off the fat in the frying pan at the end of step 1.

2 Cook the pasta following the instructions in the introduction.

3 ▲ Add the chilli powder to the bacon and cook for 2 minutes. Stir in the tomato sauce and bring to the boil. Cover and simmer for 10 minutes. Season with salt and pepper.

4 Drain the pasta thoroughly and toss it with the sauce. Serve garnished with the roughly chopped fresh parsley.

Tagliatelle with Pea and Ham Sauce

A colourful sauce, this is ideal served with crusty Italian or French bread.

SERVES 4

INGREDIENTS
350 g/12 oz tagliatelle
225 g/8 oz/1½ cups shelled peas
salt and freshly ground black pepper
300 ml/½ pint/1¼ cups single cream
50 g/2 oz/⅓ cup fontina cheese, freshly grated
75 g/3 oz Parma ham, sliced into strips

1 Cook the pasta following the instructions in the introduction.

2 Plunge the peas into a pan of boiling salted water and cook for 7 minutes or until tender. Drain.

3 ▲ Place the cream and half the fontina cheese in a small saucepan and heat gently, stirring constantly until heated through.

4 ▲ Drain the pasta thoroughly and turn it into a large serving bowl. Toss together the pasta, ham and peas and pour on the sauce. Add the remaining cheese and season with salt and pepper.

Spaghetti with Bacon, Chilli and Tomato Sauce (top), and Tagliatelle with Pea and Ham Sauce (bottom).

Penne with Chicken and Ham Sauce

A meal in itself, this colourful pasta sauce is perfect for lunch or dinner.

SERVES 4

INGREDIENTS

350 g/12 oz penne
25 g/1 oz/2 tbsp butter
1 onion, chopped
1 garlic clove, chopped
1 bay leaf
450 ml/³/4 pint/2 cups dry white wine
150 ml/¼ pint/²/3 cup crème fraîche
225 g/8 oz/1½ cups cooked chicken,
*   skinned, boned and diced*
100 g/4 oz/²/3 cup cooked lean ham, diced
100 g/4 oz/²/3 cup Gouda cheese, grated
1 tbsp chopped fresh mint
salt and freshly ground black pepper
finely shredded fresh mint, to garnish

1 Cook the pasta following the instructions in the introduction.

2 ▲ Heat the butter in a large frying pan and fry the onion for 10 minutes until softened.

3 ▲ Add the garlic, bay leaf and wine and bring to the boil. Boil rapidly until reduced by half. Remove the bay leaf, then stir in the crème fraîche and return to the boil.

4 ▲ Add the chicken, ham and cheese and simmer for 5 minutes, stirring occasionally until heated through.

5 ▲ Add the mint and seasoning.

6 ▲ Drain the pasta thoroughly and turn it into a large serving bowl. Toss with the sauce immediately, garnished with shredded mint.

COOK'S TIP

Crème fraîche is a richer, full-fat French cream with a slightly acidic taste. If you can't find any, substitute soured cream.

Short Macaroni with Ham, Tomato and Oregano Sauce

SERVES 4

INGREDIENTS
350 g/12 oz short macaroni
3 tbsp olive oil
1 beefsteak tomato, chopped
1 garlic clove, chopped
175 g/6 oz/1 cup cooked ham, cut into
*   thick strips*
175 g/6 oz/1 cup goats' cheese, diced
3 tbsp fresh oregano leaves
salt and freshly ground black pepper
goats' cheese and torn fresh oregano,
*   to garnish*

I Cook the pasta following the instructions in the introduction.

2 ▲ Heat the oil in a large frying pan and fry the tomato, garlic and ham for 3 minutes.

COOK'S TIP

Goats' cheese is available in many forms, such as in herbed oil, coated with coarsely ground pepper or plain.

3 ▲ Stir in the goats' cheese and oregano and simmer for a further 30 seconds. Season to taste.

4 Drain the pasta thoroughly and toss it with the sauce. Serve immediately, garnished with extra goats' cheese and fresh oregano.

Pasta 'Ears' with Pork in Mustard Sauce

The combination of pork and mustard give this sauce a real country taste.

SERVES 4

INGREDIENTS
350 g/12 oz pasta 'ears' (orecchiette)
4 tbsp olive oil
2 garlic cloves, chopped
350 g/12 oz pork fillet, thinly sliced
50 g/2 oz/1/4 cup butter
175 g/6 oz/2 1/2 cups flat mushrooms,
*   sliced*
1 tbsp wholegrain mustard
3 tbsp snipped fresh chives
salt and freshly ground black pepper
chopped fresh chives, to garnish

I Cook the pasta following the instructions in the introduction.

2 Heat the oil in large frying pan and fry the garlic and pork for 10 minutes, stirring occasionally until the pork is well browned and tender.

3 ▲ Add the butter, mushrooms and mustard and cook for 2 minutes, stirring occasionally. Add the chives and season to taste.

4 Meanwhile, drain the pasta thoroughly. Stir it into the pork mixture and cook for 1 minute until heated through. Serve immediately, garnished with fresh chives.

COOK'S TIP

To reduce the cost, use boneless pork chops, cut into strips.

Short Macaroni with Ham, Tomato and Oregano Sauce (top), and Pasta 'Ears' with Pork in Mustard Sauce (bottom).

Penne with Sausage and Parmesan Sauce

Spicy sausage tossed in this cheesy tomato sauce is delicious served on a bed of cooked pasta.

SERVES 4

INGREDIENTS
350 g/12 oz penne
450 g/1 lb ripe tomatoes
2 tbsp olive oil
225 g/8 oz chorizo sausage, diagonally
    sliced
1 garlic clove, chopped
2 tbsp chopped fresh flat leaf parsley
grated rind of 1 lemon
50 g/2 oz/⅓ cup Parmesan cheese,
    freshly grated
salt and freshly ground black pepper
finely chopped fresh flat leaf parsley,
    to garnish

1 Cook the pasta following the instructions in the introduction.

2 ▲ Slice the skins of the tomatoes with a knife, making a cross.

COOK'S TIP

Chorizo is quite a spicy Spanish pork sausage. A suitable Italian sausage would be salame napoletano, flavoured with red and black pepper.

3 ▲ Place the tomatoes in a large bowl, cover with boiling water and leave to stand for 30 seconds.

4 ▲ Drain the tomatoes and peel off the skins.

5 ▲ Roughly chop the tomatoes with a sharp knife.

6 ▲ Heat the oil in a frying pan and fry the sausage for 5 minutes, stirring occasionally until browned.

7 ▲ Add the tomatoes, garlic, parsley and grated lemon rind. Heat through, stirring, for 1 minute.

8 ▲ Add the Parmesan cheese and season to taste.

9 Drain the pasta thoroughly and toss it with the sauce to coat. Serve immediately, garnished with finely chopped fresh flat leaf parsley.

Tagliatelle with Chicken and Herb Sauce

This wine-flavoured sauce is best served with green salad.

SERVES 4

INGREDIENTS
2 tbsp olive oil
1 red onion, cut into wedges
350 g/12 oz tagliatelle
1 garlic clove, chopped
350 g/12 oz/2½ cups chicken, diced
300 ml/½ pint/1¼ cups dry vermouth
3 tbsp chopped fresh mixed herbs
150 ml/¼ pint/⅔ cup fromage frais
salt and freshly ground black pepper
shredded fresh mint, to garnish

1 ▲ Heat the oil in a large frying pan and fry the onion for 10 minutes until softened and the layers separate.

2 Cook the pasta following the instructions in the introduction.

3 ▲ Add the garlic and chicken to the pan and fry for 10 minutes, stirring occasionally until the chicken is browned all over and cooked through.

4 ▲ Pour in the vermouth, bring to the boil and boil rapidly until reduced by about half.

5 ▲ Stir in the herbs, fromage frais and seasoning and heat through gently, but do not boil.

6 ▲ Drain the pasta thoroughly and toss it with the sauce to coat. Serve immediately, garnished with shredded fresh mint.

COOK'S TIP

If you don't want to use vermouth, use dry white wine instead. Orvieto and frascati are two Italian wines that are ideal to use in this sauce.

Vegetable Sauces

Throughout the year in Italy, markets display an abundance of different vegetables of which the Italians make full use in their pasta dishes. The key to delicious vegetable sauces is to use really fresh produce which is full of flavour. Be adventurous with your choice of ingredients and adapt the recipes, selecting vegetables as they come into season.

Above   A vegetable stall in Padua market.

Opposite   A market scene in the Piazza dell' Erbe, Padua.

Spaghetti with Ratatouille Sauce

This is ideal to serve for vegetarians and makes a delicious alternative to any meat or fish dish.

SERVES 4

INGREDIENTS
2 tbsp olive oil
1 onion, sliced
1 clove garlic, chopped
225 g/8 oz/1½ cups courgettes, sliced
225 g/8 oz/1½ cups aubergine, halved lengthways and cut into large chunks
2 tbsp tomato purée
1 × 397 g/14 oz can chopped tomatoes
2 tbsp chopped fresh mixed herbs, such as parsley, basil, oregano
salt and freshly ground black pepper
350 g/12 oz spaghetti
fresh flat leaf parsley sprigs, to garnish
freshly grated Parmesan cheese, to serve

1 ▲ Heat the oil in a large saucepan and fry the onion for 5 minutes. Add the garlic, courgettes and aubergine and cook for 2 minutes, stirring occasionally.

COOK'S TIP

For extra colour and flavour, add sliced orange pepper when cooking the onion.

2 ▲ Stir in the tomato purée, tomatoes, herbs and seasoning and bring to the boil. Simmer for about 20–30 minutes until thickened stirring occasionally.

3 Meanwhile, cook the pasta following the instructions in the introduction. Drain thoroughly and stir it with the sauce. Toss to coat and garnish with fresh flat leaf parsley. Serve with plenty of freshly grated Parmesan cheese.

Spaghetti with Pepper and Tomato Sauce

SERVES 4

INGREDIENTS
350 g/12 oz spaghetti
2 tbsp olive oil
2 onion, chopped
1 red pepper, cored, seeded and cut into strips
1 green pepper, cored, seeded and cut into strips
1 yellow pepper, cored, seeded and cut into strips
3 tomatoes, skinned, seeded and chopped
1 garlic clove, chopped
1 tbsp chopped fresh oregano
fresh oregano sprigs, to garnish
salt and freshly ground black pepper

1 Cook the pasta following the instructions in the introduction.

2 Heat the oil in a large frying pan and fry the onions and peppers for 10 minutes until softened.

3 ▲ Stir in the tomatoes, garlic, oregano and seasoning and bring to the boil. Cover and simmer for 2 minutes.

4 Drain the pasta thoroughly and toss it with the sauce. Serve immediately, garnished with fresh oregano.

COOK'S TIP

For an even quicker sauce, use already cut pepper strips that you can buy in jars of olive oil. Fry the onion for 3–5 minutes in step 2, then drain the peppers and add them in step 3.

Spaghetti with Ratatouille Sauce (top), and Spaghetti with Pepper and Tomato Sauce (bottom).

Spaghetti with Mixed Mushroom and Basil Sauce

The combination of mixed mushroom and freshly chopped sweet basil tossed with spaghetti is well complemented by tomato salad.

SERVES 4

INGREDIENTS
50 g/2 oz/¼ cup butter
1 onion, chopped
350 g/12 oz spaghetti
350 g/12 oz/5 cups mixed mushrooms, such as brown, flat and button, sliced
1 garlic clove, chopped
300 ml/½ pint/1¼ cups soured cream
2 tbsp chopped fresh basil
50 g/2 oz/⅓ cup Parmesan cheese, freshly grated
salt and freshly ground black pepper
torn flat leaf parsley, to garnish
freshly grated Parmesan cheese, to serve

1 Melt the butter in a large frying pan and fry the onion for 10 minutes until softened.

2 Cook the pasta following the instructions in the introduction.

3 ▲ Stir the mushrooms and garlic into the onion mixture and fry for 10 minutes until softened.

4 ▲ Add the soured cream, basil, Parmesan cheese and seasoning. Cover and heat through.

5 Drain the pasta thoroughly and toss it with the sauce and garnish with torn flat leaf parsley. Serve immediately with plenty of Parmesan cheese.

Tagliatelle with Spring Vegetable Sauce

Adapt this recipe to suit your own taste. Select a combination of the vegetables recommended in the ingredients list, amounting to 300 g/12 oz in total. The rosemary will give a very Mediterranean flavour to the vegetables.

SERVES 4

INGREDIENTS
2 tbsp olive oil
100 g/4 oz baby carrots, halved lengthways
100 g/4 oz baby aubergines, halved lengthways
100 g/4 oz baby courgettes, halved lengthways
100 g/4 oz patty pan squashes (alternative)
100 g/4 oz mangetout (alternative)
100 g/4 oz baby sweetcorn (alternative)
2 garlic cloves, chopped
1 tbsp chopped fresh rosemary
300 ml/¹/₂ pint/1¹/₄ cups single cream
salt and freshly ground black pepper
350 g/12 oz tagliatelle
fresh rosemary sprigs, to garnish

1 ▲ Heat the oil in a large frying pan and fry the vegetables, garlic and rosemary over a gentle heat, covered, for 30 minutes until browned, stirring twice during cooking.

2 ▲ Remove from the heat and stir in the cream, scraping any sediment from the base of the pan. Season to taste. Return to the heat and cook for a further 4 minutes until heated through.

3 Meanwhile, cook the pasta following the instructions in the introduction.

4 Drain the pasta thoroughly and stir it into the vegetables. Serve immediately, garnished with fresh rosemary.

COOK'S TIP

Baby vegetables are available from most good greengrocers and larger supermarkets.
If you can't find any fresh rosemary, substitute ¹/₂ tbsp of dried.

Curly Spaghetti with Walnut and Cream Sauce

A classic Italian sauce with a strong, nutty flavour, this should be served with delicately flavoured salad.

SERVES 4

INGREDIENTS

350 g/12 oz curly spaghetti (fusilli col buco)
50 g/2 oz/¹/₂ cup walnut pieces
25 g/1 oz/2 tbsp butter
300 ml/¹/₂ pint/1¹/₄ cups milk
50 g/2 oz/1 cup fresh breadcrumbs
25 g/1 oz/2 tbsp Parmesan cheese, freshly grated
pinch of freshly grated nutmeg
salt and freshly ground black pepper
fresh rosemary sprigs, to garnish

I Cook the pasta following the instructions in the introduction. Meanwhile, preheat a grill.

2 ▲ Spread the walnuts evenly over the grill pan. Grill for about 5 minutes, turning them over occasionally until evenly toasted.

COOK'S TIP

Toasted walnuts add a lovely flavour to this unusual sauce, but if you prefer you can use pecan nuts as an alternative.

3 ▲ Remove from the heat, place in a clean dish cloth and rub away the skins.

4 ▲ Roughly chop the nuts.

5 ▲ Heat the butter and milk in a saucepan until the butter is melted.

6 ▲ Stir in the breadcrumbs and nuts and heat gently for 2 minutes, stirring constantly until thickened.

7 ▲ Add the Parmesan cheese, nutmeg and seasoning to taste.

8 ▲ Drain the pasta thoroughly and toss it in the sauce. Serve immediately, garnished with fresh rosemary.

Spaghetti with Pesto, Shallot and Olive Sauce

SERVES 4

INGREDIENTS
2 tbsp olive oil
225 g/8 oz/1½ cups small shallots, halved
350 g/12 oz spaghetti
1 quantity Pesto Sauce (see Pasta Spirals
  with Pesto Sauce)
75 g/3 oz/½ cup pitted black olives, halved
salt and freshly ground black pepper
torn fresh basil, to garnish

COOK'S TIP

If you make your own pesto it will keep for 2 days in the refrigerator.

1 ▲ Heat the oil in a frying pan and fry the shallots for 10 minutes until browned. Cover the pan and cook for 10 minutes over a gentle heat until softened.

2 Cook the pasta following the instructions in the introduction.

3 ▲ Stir the pesto sauce, olives and seasoning into the shallots.

4 Drain the pasta thoroughly and toss it in the sauce to coat. Serve immediately, garnished with fresh oregano leaves.

Penne with Courgette and Goats' Cheese Sauce

SERVES 4

INGREDIENTS
350 g/12 oz penne
4 tbsp olive oil
2 garlic cloves, chopped
350 g/12 oz/2 cups courgettes, sliced
225 g/8 oz/1⅓ cups herbed goats'
  cheese, diced
2 tbsp chopped fresh oregano
salt and freshly ground black pepper
shredded oregano, to garnish

COOK'S TIP

Diced feta cheese, with its sharp, salty taste, is a good alternative for goats' cheese. Only buy feta cheese that is bright white with a crumbly texture.

1 Cook the pasta following the instructions in the introduction.

2 ▲ Heat the oil in a large frying pan and cook the garlic and courgettes over a gentle heat for 10 minutes, stirring occasionally.

3 ▲ Add the goats' cheese and oregano and cook for 1 minute until heated through.

4 Drain the pasta thoroughly and stir it into the sauce. Serve immediately, garnished with flat leaf parsley.

Spaghetti with Pesto, Shallot and Olive Sauce (top), and Penne with Courgette and Goats' Cheese Sauce (bottom).

Tagliatelle with Mozzarella and Asparagus Sauce

This attractive sauce is best served with a leafy red salad.

SERVES 4

INGREDIENTS
225 g/8 oz asparagus tips
350 g/12 oz tagliatelle
100 g/4 oz/¹/₂ cup butter
1 onion, chopped
1 garlic clove, chopped
2 tbsp chicken stock or water
150 ml/¹/₄ pint/²/₃ cup double cream
75 g/3 oz/¹/₂ cup mozzarella cheese, grated
salt and freshly ground black pepper
fresh flat leaf parsley sprigs, to garnish

1 ▲ Plunge the asparagus into a pan of boiling salted water and cook for 5–10 minutes until tender. Drain.

2 Cook the pasta following the instructions in the introduction.

3 ▲ Melt the butter in a large frying pan and fry the onion for 5 minutes until softened.

4 ▲ Stir in the asparagus, garlic and chicken stock or water.

5 ▲ Stir in the cream and bring to the boil. Simmer for 2 minutes, stirring occasionally.

6 ▲ Add the mozzarella cheese and simmer for a further 1 minute. Season to taste.

7 ▲ Drain the pasta thoroughly and toss it in the sauce to coat. Serve immediately, garnished with flat leaf parsley sprigs.

COOK'S TIP

Fresh asparagus is still quite seasonal, therefore keep your eyes open and cook them in this delicious sauce when they are at their best. If you are in a hurry, use canned asparagus tips instead of fresh. Drain them well and add them in step 6.

Pasta Spirals with Mascarpone and Spinach Sauce

A creamy, green sauce tossed in lightly cooked pasta is best served with sun-dried tomato ciabatta bread.

SERVES 4

INGREDIENTS
350 g/12 oz pasta spirals (fusilli)
50 g/2 oz/¼ cup butter
1 onion, chopped
1 garlic clove, chopped
2 tbsp fresh thyme leaves
225 g/8 oz frozen spinach leaves, thawed
salt and freshly ground black pepper
225 g/8 oz/1¼ cups mascarpone cheese
fresh thyme sprigs, to garnish

1 Cook the pasta following the instructions in the introduction.

2 ▲ Melt the butter in a large saucepan and fry the onion for 10 minutes until softened.

3 ▲ Stir in the garlic, thyme, spinach and seasoning and heat gently for about 5 minutes, stirring occasionally until heated through.

4 ▲ Stir in the mascarpone cheese and heat gently until heated through.

5 Drain the pasta thoroughly and stir it into the sauce. Toss until well coated. Serve immediately, garnished with fresh thyme.

COOK'S TIP

Mascarpone is a rich Italian cream cheese. If you cannot find any, use ordinary full-fat instead.

Macaroni with Hazelnut and Coriander Sauce

This is a variation on pesto sauce, giving a smooth, herby flavour of coriander.

SERVES 4

INGREDIENTS
350 g/12 oz macaroni
50 g/2 oz/1/3 cup hazelnuts
2 garlic cloves
1 bunch fresh coriander
1 tsp salt
6 tbsp olive oil
fresh coriander sprigs, to garnish

1 Cook the pasta following the instructions in the introduction.

2 ▲ Meanwhile, finely chop the nuts.

3 ▲ Place the nuts and remaining ingredients, except 1 tbsp of the oil, in a food processor or pestle and mortar and grind together to create the sauce.

4 ▲ Heat the remaining oil in a saucepan and add the sauce. Fry very gently for about 1 minute until heated through.

5 Drain the pasta thoroughly and stir it into the sauce. Toss well to coat. Serve immediately, garnished with fresh coriander.

COOK'S TIP

To remove the skins from the hazelnuts, place them in a 180°C/350°F/Gas 4 oven for 20 minutes, then rub off the skins with a clean tea-towel.

Tagliatelle with Mixed Vegetables and Orange Sauce

This colourful sauce is delicious served with lashings of freshly grated Parmesan cheese.

SERVES 4

INGREDIENTS
50 g/2 oz/¼ cup butter
2 tbsp olive oil
2 leeks, thickly sliced
350 g/12 oz tagliatelle
115 g/4 oz/⅔ cup peas, thawed if frozen
100 g/4 oz asparagus tips
1 tbsp plain flour
grated rind and juice of 1 orange
150 ml/¼ pint/⅔ cup orange juice
salt and freshly ground black pepper

1 ▲ Melt the butter with the oil in a frying pan and fry the leeks for 5–10 minutes until almost softened.

2 Cook the pasta following the instructions in the introduction.

3 ▲ Stir the peas and asparagus tips into the leeks, cover and fry gently for about 5 minutes until slightly softened.

4 ▲ Add the flour and cook, stirring occasionally, for about 1 minute.

5 ▲ Gradually stir in the grated rind and orange juices. Return the pan to the heat and bring slowly to the boil, stirring constantly until thickened.

6 Drain the pasta thoroughly and stir it into the sauce. Toss to coat, season to taste and serve immediately.

COOK'S TIP

Other types of pasta that would be suitable for this sauce include fettucine which are thinner and pappardelle which are thicker.

Pasta Twists with Sun-dried Tomato Sauce

Sun-dried tomatoes give this sauce a truly authentic Mediterranean taste. Serve with freshly baked rolls.

SERVES 4

INGREDIENTS
350 g/12 oz pasta twists (spirali)
2 tbsp olive oil
1 red onion, thinly sliced
2 garlic cloves, chopped
1 × 190 g/7 oz jar sun-dried tomatoes in oil, drained
2 tbsp roughly chopped fresh herbs
1 × 397 g/14 oz can chopped tomatoes
50 g/2 oz/¼ cup cream cheese
salt and freshly ground black pepper
chopped fresh flat leaf parsley, to garnish

1 Cook the pasta following the instructions in the introduction.

2 ▲ Heat the oil in a frying pan and cook the onion for 5 minutes until slightly softened.

3 ▲ Add the garlic and sun-dried tomatoes and stir well.

4 ▲ Add the herbs and tomatoes and bring to the boil. Simmer for 5 minutes until sauce has thickened.

5 Drain the pasta thoroughly, set aside and keep it warm.

6 ▲ Stir the cream cheese and seasoning into the sauce and return to the boil, stirring constantly until well blended.

7 ▲ Add the pasta to the sauce, toss it to coat and serve immediately, garnished with chopped flat leaf parsley.

COOK'S TIP

Use any combination of mixed herbs. Fresh basil, flat leaf parsley and oregano will add an authentic flavour. Chives will also complement the sun-dried tomatoes.

Cut the cost of using sun-dried tomatoes in oil. Buy a large bag of dry sun-dried tomatoes from a health-food shop. Leave the tomatoes to soak overnight in water. Squeeze out the excess moisture, then put in a jar and cover with virgin olive oil. Add sliced garlic and fresh herbs for extra flavour. These will keep for several months, covered in the refrigerator.

Fish and
Seafood Sauces

*Completely surrounded by sea,
apart from the northern part, and
with well-stocked lakes, rivers and
streams, it is not surprising that fish
and seafood are regarded as staple
foodstuffs in Italy. Fish and seafood
are the perfect partner for pasta and
they often make quick, simple and
nutritious sauces suitable for any
occasion.*

Above   The fish market in Chioggia, Veneto.

Opposite   The harbour at Chioggia, Veneto.

Pasta Tubes with Tuna and Olive Sauce

A colourful Italian-style sauce, this combines well with a thicker and shorter pasta.

SERVES 4

INGREDIENTS
350 g/12 oz pasta tubes (rigatoni)
2 tbsp olive oil
1 onion, chopped
2 garlic cloves, chopped
1 × 397 g/14 oz can chopped tomatoes
50 g/2 oz/4 tbsp tomato purée
50 g/2 oz/¹/₃ cup pitted black olives,
*   quartered*
1 tbsp chopped fresh oregano
salt and freshly ground black pepper
1 × 225 g/8 oz can tuna in oil, drained
*   and flaked*
¹/₂ tsp anchovy purée
1 tbsp capers, rinsed
100 g/4 oz/²/₃ cup Cheddar cheese, grated
3 tbsp fresh white breadcrumbs
flat leaf parsley sprigs, to garnish

1   Cook the pasta following the instructions in the introduction.

2 ▲ Meanwhile, heat the oil in a frying pan and fry the onion and garlic for about 10 minutes until softened.

3 ▲ Add the tomatoes, tomato purée, and salt and pepper, and bring to the boil. Simmer gently for 5 minutes stirring occasionally.

4 ▲ Stir in the olives, oregano, tuna, anchovy purée and capers. Spoon the mixture into a serving bowl.

5 ▲ Drain the pasta, toss it well in the sauce and spoon it into flameproof serving bowls.

6 ▲ Preheat the grill and sprinkle the cheese and breadcrumbs over the pasta. Grill for about 10 minutes until the pasta is heated through and the cheese has melted. Serve immediately, garnished with flat leaf parsley.

COOK'S TIP

This speedy sauce is ideal to make when guests drop in unexpectedly because most of the ingredients are standard store cupboard items. Unopened olives packed in brine will keep for about one year.

Spaghetti with Hot-and-Sour Fish

A truly Chinese spicy taste is what makes this sauce so different.

SERVES 4

INGREDIENTS
350 g/12 oz spaghetti
450 g/1 lb monkfish, skinned
225 g/8 oz courgettes
1 green chilli, cored and seeded (optional)
1 tbsp olive oil
1 large onion, chopped
1 tsp turmeric
115 g/4 oz/⅔ cup shelled peas, thawed if
   frozen
2 tsp lemon juice
5 tbsp hoisin sauce
150 ml/¼ pint/⅔ cup water
salt and freshly ground black pepper
a sprig of dill, to garnish

1 ▲ Cook the pasta following the instructions in the introduction.

2 ▲ With a knife, cut the monkfish into bite-size pieces.

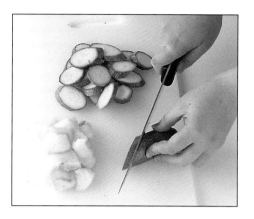

3 ▲ Thinly slice the courgettes, then finely chop the chilli.

4 ▲ Heat the oil in a large frying pan and fry the onion for 5 minutes until softened. Add the turmeric.

5 ▲ Add the chilli, courgettes and peas, and fry over a medium heat for about 5 minutes until the vegetables have softened.

6 ▲ Stir in the fish, lemon juice, hoisin sauce and water. Bring to the boil, then simmer, uncovered, for about 5 minutes or until the fish is tender. Season to taste.

7 ▲ Drain the pasta thoroughly and turn it into a serving bowl. Toss in the sauce to coat. Serve immediately, garnished with fresh dill.

COOK'S TIP

This dish is quite low in calories, therefore ideal for slimmers. Hoisin sauce is widely available from most supermarkets or Chinese stores.

Tagliatelle with Avocado, Tomato and Haddock Sauce

You will need to start this recipe the day before because the haddock should be left to marinate overnight.

SERVES 4

INGREDIENTS

350 g/12 oz fresh haddock fillets, skinned
½ tsp each ground cumin, ground
*   coriander and turmeric*
salt and freshly ground black pepper
150 ml/¼ pint/⅔ cup fromage frais
150 ml/¼ pint/⅔ cup double cream
1 tbsp lemon juice
25 g/1 oz/2 tbsp butter
1 onion, chopped
1 tbsp plain flour
150 ml/¼ pint/⅔ cup fish stock
350 g/12 oz tagliatelle
1 avocado, peeled, stoned and sliced
2 tomatoes, seeded and chopped
fresh rosemary sprigs, to garnish

I ▲ Carefully cut the haddock into bite-size pieces.

2 ▲ Mix together the spices, seasoning, fromage frais, cream and lemon juice.

3 ▲ Stir in the haddock to coat. Cover and leave to marinate overnight.

4 ▲ Heat the butter in a frying pan and fry the onion for about 10 minutes until softened. Stir in the flour, then blend in the stock until smooth.

5 ▲ Carefully stir in the haddock mixture until well blended. Bring to the boil, stirring, cover and simmer for about 30 seconds.

6 Meanwhile, cook the pasta following the instructions in the introduction.

7 ▲ Stir the avocado and tomatoes into the haddock mixture.

8 Drain the pasta thoroughly and divide it between serving plates. Spoon over the sauce and serve immediately, garnished with fresh rosemary.

COOK'S TIP

Cod and monkfish are tasty alternatives to haddock. You can also add half fresh haddock and half smoked haddock.

Seafood Spaghetti

This sauce offers a real, fresh seafood flavour. Serve with hunks of crusty French bread.

SERVES 4

INGREDIENTS
50 g/2 oz/¼ cup butter
1 onion, chopped
1 red pepper, cored, seeded and coarsely chopped
2 garlic cloves, chopped
1 tbsp paprika
350 g/12 oz spaghetti
450 g/1 lb fresh mussels
150 ml/¼ pint/⅔ cup dry white wine
2 tbsp chopped fresh parsley
225 g/8 oz peeled prawns
150 ml/¼ pint/⅔ cup crème fraîche
salt and freshly ground black pepper
finely chopped fresh flat leaf parsley, to garnish

1 Cook the pasta following the instructions in the introduction.

2 ▲ Melt the butter in a frying pan and fry the onion, pepper, garlic and paprika for 5 minutes until almost softened.

3 ▲ Rinse and scrub the mussels, making sure all the shells are tightly shut and, if not, close when tapped sharply with the back of a knife. Discard any open shells.

4 ▲ Add the wine to the pan and bring to the boil.

5 ▲ Stir in the mussels, parsley and prawns, cover and simmer for about 5 minutes until the mussels have opened. Discard any mussels that remain closed.

6 ▲ Using a slotted spoon, remove the shellfish from the pan and keep warm. Bring the juices back to the boil and boil rapidly until reduced by half.

7 ▲ Stir in the crème fraîche until well blended. Season to taste. Return the shellfish to the pan and simmer for 1 minute to heat through.

8 Drain the pasta thoroughly and divide it among the serving plates. Spoon over the shellfish and serve, garnished with finely chopped fresh flat leaf parsley.

COOK'S TIP

You can buy mixed seafood from the chill cabinets of supermarkets. Simply substitute for the mixed shellfish.

Thin Noodles with Clam, Leek and Tomato Sauce

Toss together this sauce for a real seafood flavour and serve with a light mixed salad. Canned clams make this a speedy sauce for those in a real hurry.

SERVES 4

INGREDIENTS

350 g/12 oz thin noodles (linguine)
25 g/1 oz/2 tbsp butter
2 leeks, thinly sliced
150 ml/¼ pint/⅔ cup dry white wine
4 tomatoes, skinned, seeded and chopped
pinch of ground turmeric (optional)
1 × 250 g/9 oz can clams, drained
2 tbsp chopped fresh basil
4 tbsp crème fraîche
salt and freshly ground black pepper

1 Cook the pasta following the instructions in the introduction.

2 ▲ Meanwhile, melt the butter in a small saucepan and fry the leeks for about 5 minutes until softened.

3 Add the wine, tomatoes and turmeric, bring to the boil and boil until reduced by half.

4 ▲ Stir in the clams, basil, crème fraîche and seasoning and heat through gently without boiling.

5 Drain the pasta thoroughly and toss it in the sauce. Serve immediately.

Macaroni with King Prawn, Ham and Parsley Sauce

SERVES 4

INGREDIENTS

350 g/12 oz short macaroni
3 tbsp olive oil
12 shelled raw king prawns
1 garlic clove, chopped
175 g/6 oz/1 cup smoked ham, diced
150 ml/¼ pint/⅔ cup red wine
½ small radicchio lettuce, shredded
2 egg yolks, size 3, beaten
2 tbsp chopped fresh flat leaf parsley
150 ml/¼ pint/⅔ cup double cream
salt and freshly ground black pepper
shredded fresh basil, to garnish

1 Cook the pasta following the instructions in the introduction.

2 Meanwhile, heat the oil in a frying pan and cook the prawns, garlic and ham for 5 minutes, stirring occasionally until the prawns are tender.

3 ▲ Add the wine and radicchio, bring to the boil and boil rapidly until the juices are reduced by half.

COOK'S TIP

Flat leaf parsley is a pretty herb with more flavour than the curly variety. If you buy a large bunch, finely chop the leftover parsley and freeze it in a small plastic bag. It is then ready to sprinkle onto bubbling soups or casseroles as a garnish.

4 ▲ Stir in the egg yolks, parsley and cream and bring almost to the boil, stirring constantly, then simmer until the sauce thickens slightly. Adjust the seasoning to taste.

5 Drain pasta thoroughly and toss it in the sauce to coat. Serve immediately, garnished with shredded fresh basil.

Thin Noodles with Clam, Leek and Tomato Sauce (top), and Macaroni with King Prawn, Ham and Parsley Sauce (bottom).

Stir-fried Vegetable and Prawn Sauce with Curly Spaghetti

You will need to start this recipe the day before because the prawns should be left to marinate overnight.

SERVES 4

INGREDIENTS

450 g/1 lb peeled prawns
4 tbsp/⅓ cup soy sauce
3 tbsp olive oil
350 g/12 oz curly spaghetti (fusilli col buco)
1 yellow pepper, cored, seeded and cut into strips
225 g/8 oz/1½ cups broccoli florets
1 bunch spring onions, shredded
2 cm/1 in piece fresh ginger root, peeled and shredded
1 tbsp chopped fresh oregano
2 tbsp dry sherry
1 tbsp cornflour
300 ml/½ pint/1¼ cups fish stock
salt and freshly ground black pepper

1 ▲ Place the prawns in a mixing bowl. Stir in half the soy sauce and 2 tbsp of the olive oil. Cover and marinate overnight.

2 Cook the pasta following the instructions in the introduction.

3 ▲ Meanwhile, heat the remaining oil in a wok or frying pan and fry the prawns for 1 minute.

4 ▲ Add the pepper, broccoli, spring onions, ginger and oregano and stir-fry for 1–2 minutes.

5 ▲ Drain the pasta thoroughly and set it aside and keep warm. Meanwhile, blend together the sherry and cornflour until smooth. Stir in the stock and remaining soy sauce until well blended.

6 ▲ Pour the sauce into the wok or pan, bring to the boil and stir-fry for 2 minutes until the sauce has thickened.

7 ▲ Turn the pasta into a serving bowl, pour over the sauce and toss to coat. Season to taste. Serve immediately.

COOK'S TIP

If you cannot find curly spaghetti, use other thin, long pasta such as linguine or bucatini, which looks like spaghetti but has a hole running through the centre of it.

Spaghetti with Mixed Shellfish Sauce

A special occasion sauce for an evening of entertaining is just what this is, so serve it in bountiful portions.

SERVES 4

INGREDIENTS

50 g/2 oz/¼ cup butter
2 shallots, chopped
2 garlic cloves, chopped
350 g/12 oz spaghetti
2 tbsp finely chopped fresh basil
300 ml/½ pint/1¼ cup dry white wine
450 g/1 lb mussels, scrubbed
100 g/4 oz squid, washed
1 tsp chilli powder
350 g/12 oz raw peeled prawns
300 ml/½ pint/1¼ cup soured cream
salt and freshly ground black pepper
50 g/2 oz/⅓ cup Parmesan cheese,
    freshly grated
chopped fresh flat leaf parsley, to garnish

1 ▲ Melt half the butter in a frying pan and fry 1 shallot and 1 garlic clove for 5 minutes until softened.

2 Cook the pasta following the instructions in the introduction.

3 ▲ Stir in half the basil and the wine and bring to the boil.

4 ▲ Discard any mussels that are open and do not shut when tapped with the back of a knife. Quickly add the remaining mussels to the pan, cover and simmer for about 5 minutes until all the shells have opened. Discard any mussels that do not open. Using a slotted spoon, transfer the mussels to a plate, remove them from their shells and return to the pan. Reserve a few mussels in the shells for garnishing.

5 Meanwhile, slice the squid into thin circles. Melt the remaining butter in a frying pan and fry the remaining shallot and garlic for about 5 minutes until softened.

6 ▲ Add the remaining basil, the squid, chilli powder and prawns to the pan and stir-fry for 5 minutes until the prawns have turned pink and tender.

7 ▲ Turn the mussel mixture into the prawn mixture and bring to the boil. Stir in the soured cream and season to taste. Bring almost to the boil and simmer for 1 minute.

8 Drain the pasta thoroughly and stir it into the sauce with the Parmesan cheese until well coated. Serve immediately, garnished with chopped flat leaf parsley and the reserved mussels in their shells.

COOK'S TIP

If you think raw prawns are too expensive, then use ordinary peeled prawns and add to the mixture at the end to heat through. Take care, however, that the prawns do not over-cook or they will become rubbery.

Cheese Sauces

By far the simplest way to serve pasta is with a generous grating of Parmesan cheese and olive oil, but cheeses are enjoyed throughout Italy and there are many delicious country specialities. The unusual cheeses, made locally by farmers, are rarely seen outside Italy but it is becoming increasingly easy to obtain the better-known varieties in good delicatessens and supermarkets.

Above   The cheese market in Padua.

Opposite   The Pustertal Valley, the Italian Dolomites.

Tortellini with Mushroom and Three Cheese Sauce

SERVES 4

INGREDIENTS
450 g/1 lb ricotta-and-spinach filled
   tortellini
50 g/2 oz/¼ cup butter
2 garlic cloves, chopped
225 g/8 oz/3 cups field or button
   mushrooms, sliced
15 g/½ oz/1 tbsp plain flour
175 ml/6 fl oz/¾ cup milk
50 g/2 oz/⅓ cup Parmesan cheese,
   freshly grated
50 g/2 oz/⅓ cup fontina cheese, grated
100 g/4 oz/⅔ cup ricotta cheese
4 tbsp/⅓ cup single cream
2 tbsp snipped fresh chives
salt and freshly ground black pepper

1 Cook the pasta following the instructions in the introduction.

2 ▲ Melt the butter in a large frying pan and fry the garlic and mushrooms for about 5 minutes until browned

3 Take the mushrooms out of the pan and remove the pan from the heat. Stir in the flour, then add the milk until it is absorbed by the flour.

4 Return the pan to the heat and stir in the Parmesan, fontina and ricotta cheeses and bring almost to the boil. Add the cream and chives and season to taste.

5 Drain the pasta and place it in a large serving bowl. Pour over the sauce and toss to coat. Serve immediately.

COOK'S TIP

You can use any type of mushroom in this sauce. Italians would use porcini because of their pronounced taste and that they do not loose their texture when cooked. If you can't find fresh porcini, or cep, Italian delicatessens always sell the dried variety.

Pasta Rounds with Parmesan Sauce

This is an extremely quick and simple sauce, perfect for those in a hurry.

SERVES 4

INGREDIENTS
450 g/1 lb pasta rounds (castiglioni)
50 g/2 oz/¼ cup butter
300 ml/½ pint/1¼ cups double cream
175 g/6 oz/1 cup Parmesan cheese,
   freshly grated
salt and freshly ground black pepper
2 tbsp pine nuts, toasted
finely shredded fresh flat leaf parsley,
   to garnish

1 Cook the pasta following the instructions in the introduction.

2 ▲ Heat the butter and cream together in a saucepan.

3 ▲ Stir in half the Parmesan cheese and heat gently, stirring occasionally. Keep the sauce warm.

4 Drain the pasta and turn it into a large serving bowl. Stir in the remaining Parmesan cheese and seasoning until coated. Pour over the sauce and toss to coat. Sprinkle on the pine nuts and serve immediately, garnished with parsley.

Tortellini with Mushroom and Three Cheese Sauce (top), and Pasta Rounds with Parmesan Sauce (bottom).

Pasta Spirals with Lentil and Cheese Sauce

SERVES 4

INGREDIENTS

1 tbsp olive oil
1 onion, chopped
1 garlic clove, chopped
1 carrot, cut into matchsticks
350 g/12 oz pasta spirals (fusilli)
75 g/2½ oz/½ cup green lentils, boiled
*   for 25 minutes*
1 tbsp tomato purée
1 tbsp chopped fresh oregano
150 ml/¼ pint/⅔ cup vegetable stock
225 g/8 oz/1⅓ cups Cheddar cheese,
*   grated*
salt and freshly ground black pepper
freshly grated cheese, to serve

1 ▲ Heat the oil in a large frying pan and fry the onion and garlic for 3 minutes. Add the carrot and cook for a further 5 minutes.

2 Cook the pasta following the instructions in the introduction.

3 ▲ Stir the lentils, tomato purée and oregano into the frying pan, cover and cook for 3 minutes.

4 ▲ Add the stock and salt and pepper to the pan. Cover and simmer for 10 minutes. Add the cheese.

5 Drain the pasta thoroughly and stir it into the sauce to coat. Serve with plenty of extra grated cheese.

COOK'S TIP

Tomato purée is sold in small cans and tubes. If you use a can for this small amount, you can keep the remainder fresh by transferring it to a bowl, and covering it with a thin layer of olive oil and putting it in the fridge.

Penne with Gorgonzola Sauce

Pasta tossed in a rich, creamy sauce is ideal to serve for an evening meal.

SERVES 4

INGREDIENTS

450 g/1 lb penne
50 g/2 oz/¼ cup butter
1 onion, chopped
2 celery sticks, chopped
1 garlic clove, chopped
1 tbsp chopped fresh basil
250 ml/8 fl oz/1 cup single cream
150 g/5 oz/¾ cup gorgonzola cheese, grated
225 g/8 oz/1⅓ cup mascarpone cheese
salt and freshly ground black pepper
poppy seeds, to garnish (optional)

1 Cook the pasta following the instructions in the introduction.

2 ▲ Melt the butter in a frying pan and fry the onion, celery and garlic over a gentle heat for about 10 minutes until softened, stirring occasionally. Stir in the basil and cream and heat through.

3 ▲ Pour the vegetable mixture into a food processor or liquidizer and blend until smooth.

4 Pour the sauce into the pan and bring almost to the boil, stirring occasionally. Add the gorgonzola, mascarpone, salt and pepper. Heat gently until the cheeses melt.

5 Drain the pasta thoroughly. Stir it into the sauce, tossing well to coat. Serve immediately, garnished with poppy seeds.

COOK'S TIP

Gorgonzola is a semi-soft blue-veined cheese with quite a strong flavour made in the Lombardy region of Italy. It should be creamy yellow with irregular blue veining. Do not purchase any if it is hard or has a bitter smell.

Spaghetti with Aubergine and Tomato Sauce

A recipe for a supper menu – serve this aubergine and tomato dish with freshly cooked mange-tout.

SERVES 4

INGREDIENTS
*3 small aubergines
salt and freshly ground black pepper
olive oil, for frying
450 g/1 lb spaghetti
1 quantity Classic Tomato Sauce (see
    Curly Lasagne with Classic Tomato
    Sauce)
225 g/8 oz/1⅓ cups fontina cheese, grated*

1   Top and tail the aubergines and slice them thinly.

2 ▲ Arrange the aubergine slices in a colander, sprinkling with plenty of salt between each layer. Place the colander over a plate and leave to stand for about 30 minutes.

3 ▲ Rinse the aubergines under cold running water. Drain thoroughly and pat dry on kitchen paper.

4 ▲ Heat plenty of oil in a large frying pan and fry the aubergine slices in batches for about 5 minutes, turning once during cooking until browned.

5   Meanwhile, cook the pasta following the instructions in the introduction.

6 ▲ Stir the tomato sauce into the pan with the aubergines and bring to the boil. Cover and simmer for 5 minutes.

7 ▲ Stir in the fontina cheese and salt and pepper, continue stirring over a medium heat until the cheese melts.

8   Drain the pasta and stir into the sauce, tossing well to coat.

COOK'S TIP

Supermarkets and specialist delicatessens sell hybrid baby aubergines that are ideal for using in this sauce. They are available year round. If you use these, they will brown in 3–5 minutes in step 4.

Pasta Twists with Cream and Cheese Sauce

SERVES 4

INGREDIENTS
350 g/12 oz pasta twists (spirali)
25 g/1 oz/2 tbsp butter
1 onion, chopped
1 garlic clove, chopped
1 tbsp chopped fresh oregano
300 ml/¹/₂ pint/1¹/₄ cups soured
*　cream*
75 g/3 oz/¹/₂ cup mozzarella cheese, grated
75 g/3 oz/¹/₂ cup Bel Paese cheese, grated
5 sun-dried tomatoes in oil, drained
*　and sliced*
salt and freshly ground black pepper

I Cook the pasta following the
instructions in the introduction.

2 ▲ Melt the butter in a large frying
pan and fry the onion for 10 minutes
until softened. Add the garlic and cook
for 1 minute.

COOK'S TIP

*Finely chop the leftover oregano leaves
and store in a jar of extra-virgin olive oil,
ready to use in salad dressings or other
pasta sauces.*

3 ▲ Stir in the oregano and cream and
heat gently until almost boiling. Stir in
the mozzarella and Bel Paese cheese
and heat gently, stirring occasionally
until melted. Add the sun-dried
tomatoes and season to taste.

4 Drain the pasta and turn it into a
serving bowl. Pour over the sauce and
toss well to coat. Serve immediately.

Short Pasta Tubes with Cheese and Coriander Sauce

*A speedy supper dish, this is best served
with a tomato and basil salad.*

SERVES 4

INGREDIENTS
450 g/1 lb short pasta tubes (canneroni)
100 g/4 oz full-fat garlic and herb cheese
2 tbsp very finely chopped fresh coriander
300 ml/¹/₂ pint/1¹/₄ cups single cream
salt and freshly ground black pepper
100 g/4 oz/1 cup shelled peas, cooked

I Cook the pasta following the
instructions in the introduction.

2 ▲ Melt the cheese in a small pan over
a low heat until smooth.

3 Stir in the coriander, cream, and salt
and pepper. Bring slowly to the boil,
stirring occasionally until well blended.
Stir in the peas and continue cooking
until heated through.

4 Drain the pasta and turn it into a
large serving bowl. Pour over the sauce
and toss to coat thoroughly.

COOK'S TIP

*If you do not like the pronounced flavour
of fresh coriander substitute another fresh
herb, such as basil or flat leaf parsley.*

*Pasta Twists with Cream and Cheese
Sauce (top), and Short Pasta Tubes with
Cheese and Coriander Sauce (bottom).*

Sauces for Special Occasions

You only have to go to an Italian delicatessen to see the range of authentic ingredients and delicacies that can be added to pasta sauces. In this chapter, I have used unusual ingredients that may cost more but will make your meal that much more special. Once you start experimenting with different combinations of ingredients you can create feasts fit for any occasion.

Above Grain sacks at Padua market.

Opposite Portofino, Liguria.

Tagliatelle with Smoked Salmon, Cucumber and Dill Sauce

This is a pretty pasta sauce with the light texture of the cucumber complementing the fish perfectly.

SERVES 4

INGREDIENTS
350 g/12 oz tagliatelle
1/2 cucumber
75 g/3 oz/6 tbsp butter
grated rind of 1 orange
2 tbsp chopped fresh dill
300 ml/1/2 pint/1 1/4 cup single cream
1 tbsp orange juice
salt and freshly ground black pepper
100 g/4 oz smoked salmon, skinned

1 Cook the pasta following the instructions in the introduction.

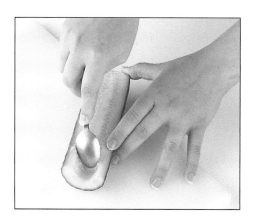

2 ▲ Using a sharp knife, cut the cucumber in half lengthways, then using a small spoon scoop out the cucumber seeds and discard.

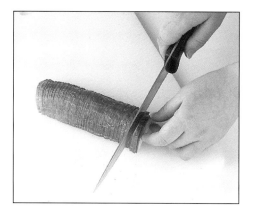

3 ▲ Turn the cucumber on the flat side and slice it thinly.

4 ▲ Melt the butter in a saucepan, add the orange rind and dill and stir well. Add the cucumber and cook gently for about 2 minutes, stirring occasionally.

5 ▲ Add the cream, orange juice and seasoning and simmer for 1 minute.

6 ▲ Meanwhile, cut the salmon into thin strips.

7 ▲ Stir the salmon into the sauce and heat through.

8 Drain the pasta thoroughly and toss it in the sauce. Serve immediately.

COOK'S TIP

An economical way to make this sauce for a special occasion is to use smoked salmon off-cuts, sold by most fishmongers and some supermarkets. Smoked trout is a less expensive alternative.

Pasta Twists with Wild Mushroom and Chorizo Sauce

The delicious combination of wild mushrooms and spicy sausage make this a tempting evening supper dish.

SERVES 4

INGREDIENTS
350 g/12 oz pasta twists (cavatappi)
4 tbsp olive oil
1 garlic clove, chopped
1 celery stick, chopped
225 g/8 oz chorizo sausage, sliced
225 g/8 oz/3 cups mixed mushrooms, such as oyster, brown cap, shiitake
1 tbsp lemon juice
2 tbsp chopped fresh oregano
salt and freshly ground black pepper
finely chopped fresh parsley, to garnish

1 Cook the pasta following the instructions in the introduction.

2 ▲ Heat the oil in a frying pan and cook the garlic and celery for 5 minutes until the celery is softened.

3 ▲ Add the chorizo and cook for 5 minutes, stirring occasionally until browned.

4 ▲ Add the mushrooms and cook for a further 4 minutes, stirring occasionally until slightly softened.

5 ▲ Stir in the remaining ingredients, except the garnish, and heat through.

6 ▲ Drain the pasta thoroughly and turn it into a serving bowl. Toss with the sauce to coat. Serve immediately, garnished with fresh parsley.

COOK'S TIP

This dish is delicious served with lashings of Parmesan cheese shavings. Use any combination of mushrooms for this flavoursome sauce.

Pasta Tubes with Scallop Sauce

A jewel from the sea such as scallop is what makes this sauce so special. Serve with a light green salad.

SERVES 4

INGREDIENTS

350 g/12 oz pasta tubes (rigatoni)
350 g/12 oz queen scallops
3 tbsp olive oil
1 garlic clove, chopped
1 onion, chopped
2 carrots, cut into matchsticks
2 tbsp chopped fresh parsley
2 tbsp dry white wine
2 tbsp Pernod
150 ml/¼ pint/⅔ cup double cream
salt and freshly ground black pepper

1 Cook the pasta following the instructions in the introduction.

2 ▲ Trim the scallops, separating the corals from the white eye part of meat.

3 ▲ Using a sharp knife, cut the eye in half lengthways.

4 ▲ Heat the oil in a frying pan and fry the garlic, onion and carrots for 5–10 minutes until the carrots are softened.

5 ▲ Stir in the scallops, parsley, wine and Pernod and bring to the boil. Cover and simmer for about 1 minute. Using a slotted spoon, transfer the scallops and vegetables to a plate and keep them warm.

6 ▲ Bring the pan juices back to the boil and boil rapidly until reduced by half. Stir in the cream and heat the sauce through.

7 ▲ Return the scallops and vegetables to the pan and heat through. Season the mixture to taste.

8 Drain the pasta thoroughly and toss it with the sauce. Serve immediately.

COOK'S TIP

The key to this sauce is not to over-cook the scallops in step 2, or they will become tough and rubbery. Frozen scallops look pure white, while fresh scallops have a creamy-grey colour.

Thin Noodles with Smoked Ham and Artichoke Sauce

SERVES 4

INGREDIENTS
350 g/12 oz thin noodles (linguine)
3 tbsp olive oil
1 onion, chopped
2 cloves garlic, chopped
1 × 397 g/14 oz can artichokes, drained
*   and sliced*
225 g/8 oz/1⅓ cups Italian-style smoked
*   ham, diced*
2 tbsp chopped fresh basil
1 tbsp herb vinegar
salt and freshly ground black pepper
150 ml/¼ pint/⅔ cup soured cream
fresh mint sprigs, to garnish

1 Cook the pasta following the instructions in the introduction.

2 ▲ Heat the oil in a frying pan and fry the onion and garlic for 5 minutes. Add the artichokes.

COOK'S TIP

Use ordinary ham if you prefer. Smoked chicken is also delicious in this recipe.

3 ▲ Cook the artichokes for 2 minutes, then add the ham and basil and fry, stirring, for 2 minutes. Add the herb vinegar and seasoning and heat through. Stir in the cream and heat through again.

4 Drain the pasta thoroughly and toss it with the sauce. Serve immediately, garnished with fresh mint.

Penne with Anchovy and Broccoli Sauce

SERVES 4

INGREDIENTS
350 g/12 oz penne
4 tbsp olive oil
1 clove garlic, chopped
1 red onion, chopped
2 tbsp pine nuts
1 × 50 g/2 oz can anchovies
225 g/8 oz/1⅓ cups broccoli florets
salt and freshly ground black pepper

COOK'S TIP

Anchovies are very salty, so for those who don't like too much salt, soak the anchovies in milk for 30 minutes before chopping. Taste the sauce before seasoning.

1 Cook the pasta following the instructions in the introduction.

2 Heat the oil in a saucepan and fry the garlic, onion and pine nuts for 5 minutes until softened.

3 ▲ Chop the anchovies and stir into the onion mixture, including the oil from the tin. Cook gently for 1 minute, mashing the anchovies slightly with the back of a wooden spoon.

4 ▲ Stir in the broccoli, cover and simmer for 5 minutes until the broccoli is tender. Stir in the seasoning.

5 Drain the pasta thoroughly and toss it in the sauce. Serve immediately.

Thin Noodles with Smoked Ham and Artichoke Sauce (top), and Penne with Anchovy and Broccoli Sauce (bottom).

Tagliatelle with Parma Ham, Asparagus and Cheese Sauce

A stunning sauce, this is worth every effort to serve for a special occasion evening meal.

SERVES 4

INGREDIENTS
350 g/12 oz tagliatelle
25 g/1 oz/2 tbsp butter
1 tbsp olive oil
225 g/8 oz asparagus tips
1 garlic clove, chopped
100 g/4 oz Parma ham, sliced into strips
2 tbsp chopped fresh sage
150 ml/¼ pint/⅔ cup single cream
100 g/4 oz Chive-and-Onion double
    Gloucester cheese, grated
100 g/4 oz/⅔ cup Gruyère cheese, grated
salt and freshly ground black pepper
fresh sage sprigs, to garnish

1 Cook the pasta following the instructions in the introduction.

2 ▲ Melt the butter and oil in a frying pan and gently fry the asparagus tips for about 5 minutes, stirring occasionally until almost tender.

3 ▲ Stir in the garlic and Parma ham and fry for 1 minute.

4 ▲ Stir in the sage leaves and fry for a further 1 minute.

5 ▲ Pour in the cream and bring to the boil.

6 ▲ Add the cheeses and simmer gently, stirring occasionally until thoroughly melted. Season to taste.

7 ▲ Drain the pasta thoroughly and toss it with the sauce to coat. Serve immediately, garnished with fresh sage.

Thin Noodles with Sweet Pepper and Cream Sauce

SERVES 4

INGREDIENTS

1 orange pepper, cored, seeded and cubed
1 yellow pepper, cored, seeded and cubed
1 red pepper, cored, seeded and cubed
350 g/12 oz thin noodles (linguine)
2 tbsp olive oil
1 red onion, sliced
1 garlic clove, chopped
2 tbsp chopped fresh rosemary
150 ml/¼ pint/⅔ cup double cream
salt and freshly ground black pepper
fresh rosemary sprigs, to garnish

1 Preheat the grill to hot.

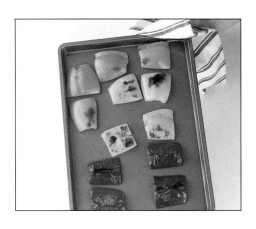

2 ▲ Place the peppers skin sides up on a grill rack. Grill for 5–10 minutes until the pepper skins begin to blister and char.

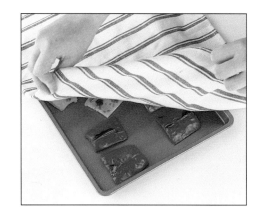

3 ▲ Remove the peppers from the heat, cover with a clean dish towel and leave to stand for 5 minutes.

4 ▲ Carefully peel away the skins from the peppers and discard. Slice the peppers into thin strips.

5 Cook the pasta following the instructions in the introduction.

6 ▲ Heat the oil in a frying pan and fry the onion and garlic for about 5 minutes until softened.

7 ▲ Stir in the peppers and rosemary and fry gently for about 5 minutes until heated through.

8 ▲ Stir in the cream and heat through gently. Season to taste.

9 Drain the pasta thoroughly and toss in the sauce. Serve immediately, garnished with fresh rosemary.

COOK'S TIP

Be sure to char the pepper skins all over for easy skinning. If you have a gas hob, spear the peppers and hold them over the flame until they are charred all over.

Mixed Summer Pasta

A pretty colourful sauce with bags of flavour makes this a dish for the summer.

SERVES 4

INGREDIENTS
350 g/12 oz curly spaghetti (fusilli col buco)
100 g/4 oz french beans, cut into 2.5 cm/ 1 in pieces
salt and freshly ground black pepper
2 tbsp olive oil
½ fennel bulb, sliced
1 bunch spring onions, sliced diagonally
100 g/4 oz yellow cherry tomatoes
100 g/4 oz red cherry tomatoes
2 tbsp chopped fresh dill
225 g/8 oz peeled prawns
1 tbsp lemon juice
1 tbsp wholegrain mustard
4 tbsp soured cream
fresh dill sprigs, to garnish

I ▲ Cook the beans in a saucepan of boiling salted water for about 5 minutes until tender. Drain.

2 Cook the pasta following the instructions in the introduction.

3 ▲ Heat the oil in a frying pan and fry the fennel and spring onions for about 5 minutes.

4 ▲ Stir in the cherry tomatoes and fry for a further 5 minutes, stirring occasionally.

5 ▲ Add the dill and prawns and cook for 1 minute.

6 ▲ Stir in the lemon juice, mustard, soured cream, seasoning and beans and simmer for 1 minute.

7 Drain the pasta and toss with the sauce. Serve immediately, garnished with fresh dill.

COOK'S TIP

Yellow cherry tomatoes are not always in season, so simply substitute with red cherry tomatoes.

Index